Kevin,
Here's to Authentic Leadership
My friend! Than,
Support the Year

Authentic Leadership Development:
Access to Breakthrough Performance

THE FUNDAMENTALS

Pauline Serice

BREAKTHROUGH POSSIBILITY PUBLISHING
WWW.PAULINESERICE.COM

First Edition

Copyright © 2011 by Pauline Serice & Associates, Inc.
Breakthrough Possibility Publishing
www.paulineserice.com

Printed and bound in the U.S.A.

Library of Congress Cataloging-in-Publication Data
Serice, Pauline
Authentic Leadership Development: Access to Breakthrough
Performance – The Fundamentals/ Pauline Serice – 1st ed.

ISBN 978-0-9839021-0-2

1. Leadership. 2. Business. 3. Psychology. 4. Self-
Development.

CONTENTS

Track I - The Psychology & Philosophy of ALD

Track II - The Practical Application of ALD

Dedication

People are often unreasonable, illogical and self-centered;
forgive them anyway.
If you are kind, people may accuse you of selfish, ulterior motives;
be kind anyway.
If you are honest and frank, people may cheat you;
be honest and frank anyway.
What you spend years building, someone could destroy overnight;
build anyway.
If you find sincerity and happiness, they may be jealous;
be happy anyway.
The good you do today, people will often forget tomorrow;
do good anyway.
Give the world your best anyway. You see, in the final analysis, it is
between you and God;
It was never between you and them anyway.

Mother Theresa

Acknowledgments

I would like to acknowledge my Lord and Savior Jesus Christ for giving me the courage and belief through His infinite Grace that I have a voice worth sharing in this life.

I would also like to sincerely acknowledge all of my amazing clients who throughout the years have relentlessly encouraged me amidst every challenge and seemingly immovable impasse, to do this work "anyway". In particular I would like to thank a very special person, Ben Klingbeil, who has not only been one of my most *transformed* clients but also has become my dearest friend. Your confidence in the mission that I am on and your unshakeable support of me as a human being has been immeasurable. With all my heart, *Thank You!*

Preface

I have written this book in a humble attempt to provide a useful conversation and fundamental working guide for the unique person who seeks to be an authentic leader in his or her life. From the Greek's mandate to "know thyself" to Aristotle's conception of a life with meaning necessarily is a life lived upon "self-truth", this book addresses modern day issues in developing one's self as an authentic leader first and foremost and by virtue of this primary mandate, seeks to spark the resurrection of authentic leadership in our organizations and institutions. The notion of the importance of the authentic self in living a fulfilling life has throughout history been a subject of enormous philosophical and psychological interest and attention. I am most certainly a fully engaged member of this group of fascinated inquirers.

Based on my experiences over the past 25 years via my own personal development, academic endeavors and professional work with thousands of clients, these pages represent the fundamentals of an articulated point of view as to what I have witnessed and therefore believe to be an effective foundation for Authentic Leadership Development (ALD). I have created a "twin track" approach, which incorporates both the psychological (which includes the philosophical) and the practical. The psychological track addresses removing the roadblocks that I have found most often impede the transformational process of becoming an authentic leader. These include excessive self-doubt, procrastination, self-righteous arrogance, self-deprecation, excessive fear and anxiety. This ALD process is essentially about becoming aware of, examining, and modifying problematic thinking and subsequent ineffective "being" in the world. The practical track deals with the reality of creating and accomplishing a clearly defined "breakthrough" project to execute goals and actions consistent with an authentic leader's true self. This enormously important track acts as a "learning laboratory" through which authentic leadership concepts and principles are applied and developed.

It is important to point out that one track without the other is insufficient to forward the prospect of becoming an authentic leader and producing breakthrough results. Following a well thought out and flexibly adaptable plan encompassed in a breakthrough project leads to the application of ALD psychological and philosophical principles and the subsequent self-actualization of authentic leadership into breakthrough performance. Therefore dealing with both the psychological and the practical is equally and essentially important. I'm also introducing a new term into the leadership development lexicon, that of "_existential_ leadership coaching" whose aim is to enhance the leader's capacity for being self-reflective and to forward that leader's ability to impact their perspective for the purpose of becoming more effective and feeling a deepened sense of accomplishment in his or her work and life.

One final note, if there is anything in these pages, which causes you to get "upset" or angry with me, my first suggestion is to stop and consider whatever that is as a key **opportunity** to transform something in your life (i.e., what we resist persists). In fact, my thinking is that if the reading of this book "_does not_" make you uncomfortable to some degree then I have not succeeded in doing my job, which is to provoke and inspire you to actually *do something differently*! In order for that to happen, we have to be humble enough to see our current modus operandi as insufficient to fulfill on what we truly desire out of this life. My second suggestion is, if the first suggestion doesn't seem to work or doesn't interest you and you find that you are still upset and angry with me, "let it go"... in the final analysis, this is only my point of view anyway! Please feel free to make me wrong and to be right if that ultimately works for you. Wishing you all the best on your personal journey of authentic leadership!

Pauline Serice
Houston, TX
August 2011

Introduction

I sincerely appreciate you joining me in being committed to exploring the conversation of Authentic Leadership Development. I have to say that I love this subject and I believe that it is so important to our society that I am personally dedicated to the resurrection of authentic leadership in our organizations and institutions. As an executive coach, organizational consultant and scientific researcher, I have found over the years that leaders at all levels and in all types of organizations are increasingly facing the soul wrenching challenge of declining hope and confidence in themselves and their associates. There appears to be a fundamental breakdown in our society of true leadership. I believe that authenticity—or, more precisely the lack of it—lies near the heart of this crisis in confidence. I also believe and have experienced through 25 years of focused development on myself and facilitating the development of others that being yourself: being the person you were created to be *rather than* developing a style or image or persona of a leader is the kind of leadership that CAN restore confidence.

Within these pages, I will share with you what I have come to realize is the foundation of what it takes to start and to sustain this developmental journey. The time we spend is not meant to be an "intellectual exercise" but rather my intention is that we start to confront and grapple with issues that address developing ourselves in becoming more authentic in practice in our day-to-day accountabilities.

I'll be introducing concepts that will expand on more fully...

> ➤ What it means to be an authentic leader
>
> ➤ How one might begin that journey

➤ The main road blocks which seem to stop people and

➤ Where to go to work removing these blocks to cause breakthroughs in performance

What does it mean to be an authentic leader? Leadership can be characterized as establishing direction, aligning people, and inspiring movement to overcome inevitable obstacles encountered along the way. One approach to understanding authenticity is contrasting it with sincerity - while sincerity is honesty when sharing your thoughts and feeling with others, authenticity in contrast is being honest or true to oneself. Many leaders think they are being authentic when in actuality they are just being right about their opinion and regurgitating that "dug in" positional opinion onto anyone who will listen. This way of operating is very distinct from authenticity as it is presented here. That is to say, being right about what you think while making others wrong is not being an authentic leader.

Fundamental characteristics of authentic leaders include being genuine and not fake, not being pressured by society to act as if you're something you are not and being committed to a cause or mission bigger than the maintenance of your ego. Authenticity refers to owning one's personal experience, be they thoughts, emotions, needs, wants, preferences, beliefs and operating consistently with one's "true self". Namely, expressing oneself in ways that are consistent with one's values, inner thoughts, feelings and commitments.

Can you guess what the single most requested organizational intervention that I as a consultant am asked into a company for is? ... "To positively impact trust and collaboration." Leaders today have been placed under unprecedented demands to produce results, which are critically affected by high levels of mistrust and lack of collaboration. With the movement in organizations going from capital-intensive activities requiring highly efficient machine and human processes to knowledge-intensive, team-based activities requiring high levels of trust and collaboration, for all intents and purposes today's leaders are woefully unprepared to handle these complex human issues while under such pressure to continuously produce challenging results. Thankfully, authentic leadership has been shown to create these critically needed levels of trust. I believe this is because the essence of authentic leadership seems to be derived from a person's sincere grappling with a very fundamental human question regarding one's own existence, that is...

How Shall I Live My Life?

1

How Shall I Live My Life?

"How shall I live my life?" given the fundamental conditions human beings find themselves while operating inside of organizations. When an authentic leader takes responsibility for answering this question, they have to sincerely deal with the very nature of their own existence and how that existence is manifested in their day-to-day living. This forces the person committed to being an authentic leader to strip away what isn't real and genuine and behave consistently with **what is** genuine and **what is** real. Authentic leaders are effective in leading others because followers look for this consistency.

Because of this, I orient Authentic Leadership Development (ALD) as _a self-actualizing and progressive state based upon the leader's development of his or her authentic sense of self and the relationship between that sense of self and their actions._ I say this based on the fact that the leader role is highly challenging and requires a high level of self-motivation, commitment, innovation, strategic thinking and persistence. To lead effectively, especially when leadership involves organizational change or providing coaching and guidance, people need to overcome natural human resistance, enroll others for support, navigate frustrations and setbacks, make personal sacrifices, and truly engage themselves and others. Dealing with these challenges requires a powerful internal compass to stay the course. Summoning the will to lead and the energy to overcome obstacles and inevitable difficulties requires a leader to operate from clearly articulated values, convictions and a strong sense of self. The question: "How shall I live my life?" is answered not only in the ideas people have of themselves in their head but also in the practical way a person actually translates those ideas of himself or herself into constructing life day-to-day. To *be* an authentic leader requires everyday day-in day-out courage.

Often this sort of conversation is dismissed as too philosophical for practical application. Right now you may be saying to yourself, "Ok, this is a nice theoretical conversation but at some point I have to go back and get some **real** work done!" This is an understandable reaction of human anxiety and resistance to genuinely addressing very complex and confronting questions regarding the purpose of our existence and facing whether or not we are truly being that person in the world. However, if we honestly take a hard look at what is happening in our economy and society in general today, the literal implosion of major institutions due to massive ethical deterioration in the executive ranks followed by all levels of organizations feeling justified in mirroring the attitudes and behaviors of these so called "leaders", I've come to the conclusion that's it's pretty naïve at best and egregiously irresponsible at worst NOT to finally start addressing these issues openly and with a focused intention to resolving them. Something clearly has to be done, and continuing to do what we've done in the past, expecting a different result is well, as we all know...INSANITY!

I believe what I do and who I am being in this world matters. I also believe the same is true for you. Do you believe that? Are you _willing_ to believe that and _do something_ about it? If so, as a leader how do we start to answer the fundamental existential question, "How shall I live my life?" First we have to become familiar with what I call the modus operandi of authentic leaders...

2

Modus Operandi of Authentic Leaders

What really
am I about?

What truly
am I
committed
to?

Self-Reflective

Self-Actualize
Leadership

Strong Sense
of Self

Who
am I?

Goals Manifest
the Self

Conversations &
Behavior Express
the Self

I've found over the years working with and developing hundreds of leaders committed to being authentic, including myself, that there seems to be a consistent pattern of operating that authentic leaders commit themselves to developing. This pattern includes being highly self-reflective, having a strong sense of self, expressing the self in their consistent conversations and behavior, manifesting the self through clearly articulated goals and self-actualizing leadership. As you can see, this type of leadership is not focused on typical leadership development categories (those focused on doing specific behaviors differently or learning new skills) but rather, it is fundamentally about the development of the authentic self and questioning one's own existence by addressing existential questions in life. Namely, "Who am I?" "What really am I about?" and, "What truly am I committed to?" Then actually, expressing these commitments in the world through clearly articulated and acted upon goals.

Without truly answering these questions and being guided by those answers, I have found that people in leadership accountabilities quickly lose their way when faced with the inevitable pressures of consistently producing demanding results. While I have literally never met a leader who didn't believe that being authentic was direly needed in his or her organization, authentic leadership for many of those same leaders, by their own admission, lives as "a good idea", "purely a concept" or "a self-indulgent philosophical luxury", not a practical and essentially practiced day-to-day process of "_being_" manifested in the world in which they inhabit. I realized through my experiences of working with these people that resigned beliefs such as those noted above originated from the fact that the person just didn't know _how_ to develop themselves for accomplishing authenticity consistently. Our society does not teach such things in our school systems and frankly even the prospect of believing one could truly be authentic consistently in this façade ridden and cordially duplicitous world is initially somewhat overwhelming to fathom. To counteract this feeling of overwhelm, their strategy typically is to put the possibility of being an authentic leader down as an unrealistic fantasy and go about "doing the best that they can" given the gut wrenching and soul diminishing circumstances they have been dealt. After all that is the more "reasonable" thing to do, right? It's this way "everywhere" so why should it be different here?

This is the gap in leadership development I am dedicated to transforming, i.e., restoring hope and confidence in the possibility of authentic leadership in our organizations and institutions by providing a sustainable process through which one can develop ones' "self" in becoming an authentic leader. Therefore, if you are truly committed to being an authentic leader, let's take a look at what each of the components of this modus operandi is made   up   of.

Authentic Leadership Development

Self-Reflective

Who am I?

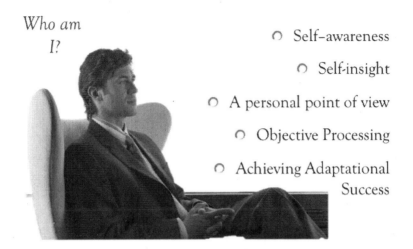

○ Self–awareness

○ Self-insight

○ A personal point of view

○ Objective Processing

○ Achieving Adaptational Success

"Who am I?" ... To be self-reflective and "know-oneself", one needs to seriously ponder this question. Being true to "self", mandates that you know who this "self" is; self-awareness is required if you are to determine what is distinctly your own. Self-awareness reveals the leaders unique purpose in this life. To find your purpose you have to explore and understand yourself, your particular passions, and your fundamental motivations. Through the self-reflective process, I suggest gathering self-insights, which help articulate your purpose in a concisely written statement. For example, my purpose is, "To instruct and inspire in a worthwhile and positive manner, ultimately increasing the quality of peoples' lives." I align my choices in this life to that purpose. Through examining your "self" you find your "voice". What do you really think and know about your "self" and the world around you? The more self-aware you become the more alive you are.

Frequently the desired outcome of leadership development is sustained alterations in behavior. The leader is typically charged with demonstrating a significant transformation of ineffective behavior even when confronted with adverse situations and pressure. A substantial portion of the literature supports that resistance to these alterations is primarily psychological in nature. Lasting shifts in behavior tend to be frustrated, avoided, and resisted by a myriad of habitual conversations, schemas (a fancy word for mental models), fundamental assumptions, attitudes and beliefs, unconscious defense mechanisms, and overly exaggerated subjective and internal dialogues. Everything I have learned over the years as a professional consultant and executive coach aligns with this premise, therefore I believe that truly sustainable leadership development with subsequent "transformation" in behavior requires critical shifts in deep intra-psychic processes connected to a person's sense of self. Individuals left to their own devices typically do not possess the knowledge, skill or ability to identify nor access these complex processes. The result being that, people have enormous difficulty achieving and sustaining long-term fundamental change in behavior.

Clearly, at the deepest level, authentic leaders must deal with their very complex, emotional and often paradoxical natures by significantly improving levels of self-reflection and self-awareness. This seems to be why executive coaching with a professional possessing practical experience and academic training in the three critical areas of leadership coaching psychology, organizational development and business acumen has gained such popularity over the past ten years. Often leaders become much more successful when they work with this type of experienced professional who can assist them in addressing the challenges of becoming self-reflective, self-aware, and open to continuous learning and development of the self, their organizational dynamics, and ultimately connecting these insights to business performance.

Higher levels of self-reflective ability also contribute to an authentic leader being original and not "fake". While authentic leaders are not necessarily uniquely different from each other in their competencies or personality traits and the content of their values, convictions, cause or mission could very well appear to be the same as others, the process through which they have arrived at these convictions and causes is not a process of "fabrication". They have internalized their values and convictions on the basis of their own personal experiences and emotions. They take the risks they need to take to engage in their own individual experiences and therefore literally "own" these experiences. This ownership dictates a quality of "being" unmistakably recognizable as an authentic point of view.

Leadership without this personalized perspective and point of view isn't leadership. One cannot simply "parrot" a point of view read out of a leadership book or heard from another person and expect it to be listened to with any amount of conviction. The authentic leader must "own" it, and you "own it" by having experienced it to be true! Your point of view doesn't have to be different from others, but it does need to be personal in the sense that it has developed from your personal experience, personal awareness and personal exploration. Let me make this perfectly clear, you will not become an authentic leader by reading the concepts in this book and not **doing anything** differently or not **being** differently.

A Strong Sense of Self

Where are you headed? Our psychological universe as human beings revolves around our fundamental view of ourselves. You may get away with "passing the buck" or "making other people wrong" during the day but in the middle of the night, when you are all alone and have to look at yourself in the mirror, you

must reconcile whether you truly view yourself as being a person **who is committed to** "passing the buck" and "making others wrong". If you are not, then behaving inconsistently with who you **believe yourself to be** in your heart and soul will create continuous psychological tension, distress and confusion. Self-views and self-beliefs create the context for all other knowledge. Having a strong sense of self calls for the leader's self-views, self-knowledge, values and deeply held convictions to be clearly and confidently defined and internally consistent. To clarify and construct a strong sense of self, one must develop an equally sound ability to concentrate.

Concentration is the opposite of distraction. It is focusing one's attention on a single issue to the exclusion of others. Without concentration there can be no capacity for life. Without concentration one cannot learn. Until one acquires the capacity to truly concentrate on the development of his or her self-beliefs and values, becoming an authentic leader will seem like an overwhelming, tedious and insurmountable task. It is in the experience of deep concentration that the consciousness is unusually well ordered. The self becomes more stable and complex as a result of clearly developing one's self-beliefs, values and convictions. It is by learning how to become increasingly complex that the strong sense of self emerges. If you cannot sustain mental focus and develop this complexity, you will have an unstable sense of self.

Complexity is often thought of in a negative connotation, consistent with something that is difficult or confusing. However, here I am speaking of complexity as the result simply of differentiation and integration. Differentiation implies developing one's own self-beliefs and values and distinguishing what is personal about these in contrast to others. Integration is characterized by how that self is relationally integrated with the interdependencies of others. A "complex" self is merely one that is successful in combining these seemingly paradoxical concepts, becoming an individual who is uniquely you while also connecting with others as a part of a larger whole.

- ○ Self-beliefs & values clearly and confidently defined
- ○ Internally consistent
- ○ Stable sense of self-knowledge

Caution! This notion of distinguishing and developing your self-beliefs, values and deeply held convictions can quickly devolve into an "exercise". It is for this reason that I have put such an emphasis on concentration while forming this key aspect of authentic leadership development. The simple act of choosing to invest ourselves to the limits of our concentration while distinguishing our self-beliefs, values and convictions builds a level of clarity about our self which bolsters self-confidence that allows for the development and expression of a stronger emerging sense of self.

Conversations and Behavior Express the Self

Authentic leaders are leaders whose actions are motivated by their values and convictions. They are inspired by their commitments and convictions rather than simply having an "If I do this for you then what's in it for me?" orientation. Their conversations are consistent with what they believe, and their actions are consistent with both their conversations and their beliefs.

They regulate their conversations and behavior in ways that satisfy their internal compass, thus satisfying the basic psychological needs for competence, self-determination and relatedness. Because they act in accordance to their values and beliefs rather than ulterior motives (e.g., you don't "call me" on my stuff and I won't "call you" on yours), authentic leaders are often characterized as having a high level of integrity. In contrast, self-regulation driven by **external** expectations or demands is associated with a lack of integrity. For example, when one's actions are primarily motivated by personal concerns of "looking good", "political correctness" and "personal advancement" at the expense of what is best for employee

- ○ Motivated by values and convictions

- ○ Talk and action are an expression of purpose and values

- ○ High level of integrity

- ○ Highly transparent

engagement, effective organizational performance and sustainable competitive advantage in one's industry.

Because authentic leaders' conversations and behavior are consistent with their beliefs and values, they can also be described as being highly transparent. Authentic leaders stay acutely aware of their weaknesses and potential "blind spots" and openly discuss them with associates. They don't try to pretend to be "bullet proof" and this is demonstrated in their behavior of being transparent. Leaders committed to being authentic responsibly concentrate on developing their areas of weakness to their fullest potential.

Goals Manifest the Self

Authentic leaders are motivated by goals that reflect, "Who they really are". In contrast, goals not in alignment with a leader's sense of self are ones that are pursued with an attitude of "having to". In this scenario, the person does not really perceive the goals as their own nor do they necessarily believe in them. Authentic leaders do not take on a leadership role or engage in leadership goals for status, honor, or other personal rewards. While they may consider financial gains relatively important and appreciate the impact advantage of occupying a position with decision-making authority, their basic orientation is to lead from strongly held values and convictions. Goals encapsulate a value-based cause or mission, and to engage in leadership is to fulfill on this cause or mission.

○ Goals are actual passions

○ Goals represent central values and beliefs

They are fully engaged in their own self-actualization and are interested not only in being all that they can be but also in making a difference with others. Authentic leaders are people who pursue life goals with a sense that these goals express their authentic choices rather than externally imposed duties or conventions. There also appears to be something unique about the relationship between core elements of the self and the authentic leader's experience of meaning in life. Meaning for these leaders is not obtained simply from performing a job or function well, but from feeling that one is in touch with and enacting goals that are expressions of who they believe themselves to be. In other words the authentic leader is motivated by internal commitment, which in the end analysis is a commitment to a sense of self.

CPSIA information can be obtained at www.ICGtesting.com
Printed in the USA
LVOW040844141211

259269LV00001B/18/P

Self-Actualize Leadership

Finally, authentic leaders do not fake their leadership. Accepting a leadership position is not simply a decision they came to in order to amass more money or wield more power and status. They do not pretend to be leaders just because they are in a leadership position. Nor do they work on developing an image, style, or persona of a leader. Rather, performing a leadership function and related activities are self-expressive acts for authentic leaders. It is part of what they feel to be their "true" or "real" self.

○ The leader role is not what you do it's **who you are**.

An authentic leader does not necessarily have to occupy the highest-level leadership position or for that matter occupy a formal leadership position at all to define themself as a leader. They may even use other terms to refer to themself such as a "business partner" or "champion for a cause" however they think of themself in terms of a leader and enact that role at all times, not only when they are officially "in the role" whether formal or informal. That is to say, when enacting the leadership role, authentic leaders are being themselves (as opposed to conforming to others' expectations). Being a leader is simply "who they are". They can't, "not lead". It is in the fiber of their "being".

Given this modus operandi which authentic leaders are committed to putting into existence in their everyday lives, the next important question becomes...

Are you truly "being" an authentic leader or are you just _playing one_ on TV?

I want you to take a moment and reflect on what you have read so far. Related to the modus operandi you were just introduced to, jot down below where in your life or specifically at work you have not been being the authentic leader you would like to be or even more precisely the leader that you are committed to being.

3

Why Do We Get Stopped?

Why do we get stopped from being the authentic leader we say we are committed to being? I have found we get stopped primarily due to how we have constructed what I call our <u>"Self-and-World View"</u> to function in life. A self-and-world view can be defined as what we have decided about the world and ourselves. That is, individuals understand the world on the basis of their unique psychological and social construction of reality. This self-and-world view is how people survive, seek fulfillment, and avoid harm. For example, one person may "see" a situation and interpret it as "the glass half full", while another person "sees" and interprets the <u>same</u> situation as "the glass half empty". Each person has "constructed" his or her own view of himself or herself and of the world differently in this example. But for each person, their view tends to "live" like **THE TRUTH** about the world and themselves not simply a point of view, which could be one of many.

And, for the most part human beings' "world view" is that, there _is_ a world "_out there_", separate from them, which "stops" them from being the kind of leader they say they want to be or having

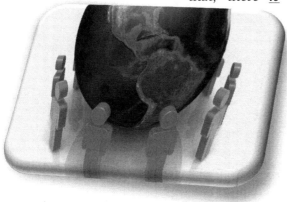

the kind of life they say they want to have. In addition, they accumulate explanations and reasonable justifications as evidence to prove to anyone who will take the time to listen, why this terrible situation or world "out-there" beyond their control is stopping them. In fact, they spend an inordinate amount of time _talking about why_ **they can't** reach their goals, as opposed to actually _working on_ reaching their goals. I assert that what they are experiencing is not a world "out-there" stopping them, but rather A Crisis of Perception...

Being an Inauthentic "Leader"
A Crisis of Perception

Being an inauthentic "leader" (a bit of an oxymoron) is typically the product of a person who has lost their belief that they can make any difference. They feel as though they have been pushed around to the extent that they have become lost in the experience of making their own way. They've thrown their hands up and decided to just play the unwinnable game...and if nobody else is going to care enough to do anything differently then neither are they (now their self-and-world view). This can manifest itself in feeling powerless to protect oneself, being swamped and petrified by fear and doubt and generally being swept along on a day-in day-out basis never really knowing what it feels like to have a strong sense of accomplishment and to be connected with others and feel truly alive and part of something.

Every leader has faced looking into this abyss at one time or another. Regaining our ability, in the midst of this despair, to deliberately intervene in our own lives and live according to our own inner wisdom requires constant commitment to being personally courageous. So if we are willing to be personally courageous and are truly committed to being authentic leaders, how then can we obliterate this overwhelm and despair? We do it by gaining access to *shifting* our perception of the current situation, which is in fact sourced by our current limiting self-and-world view. To do this, one must first understand the components that make up this view....

Your Background of Reality

At a practical level, exploring one's personal meaning structures gives access to distinguishing the self-and-world view. These meaning structures include one's beliefs, assumptions, judgments, interpretations, assessments, values and self-perceptions. The interrelationships of these structures constitute a person's fundamental "being" and behavior in the world. The self-and-world view becomes one's **Background of Reality**. It alters what we see, say and do often without our being aware of it. It is a constructed "bubble" of sorts that we as human beings occupy which encapsulates us **inside** of our assumptions, judgments, assessments, interpretations, beliefs and values. This bubble protects us in a world that we perceive is dangerous, that we need protection from and it has us feel more comfortable by creating a world that is familiar to us that we can be "right" about.

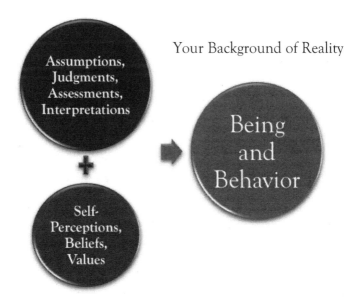

27

Unfortunately, what we don't realize more times than not is that the very bubble we have constructed to protect us, often times is actually **imprisoning us**. If we want to transform our being and behavior in the world, i.e., notice and limit our inauthenticity, we need to identify our current *limiting* assumptions, beliefs, values, judgments, etc., These *limiting paradigms* are at the source of the inauthentic being and behavior and have us "give up" due to the belief that we can't make a difference. Our **background of reality** needs to be transformed if significant shifts in being an authentic leader are to be achieved. But how do we do that in a way that is practical to our day-to-day life so that it doesn't occur like its just positive thinking in an individual vacuum when everyone else is seemingly thinking another way?????...

4

Self-and-World View
A Communication Driven Phenomenon

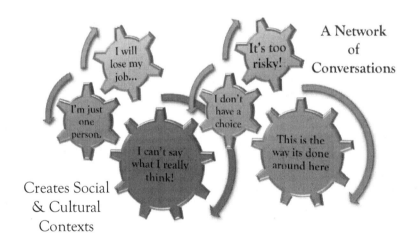

We can transform our background of reality by understanding the self-and-world view as a communication driven phenomenon. Most people will talk about communication in a very ordinary manner as a mundane way of conveying information or as a tool for change. I maintain the opposite: that communication is extraordinarily powerful and that change or what I call "transformation" is a phenomenon that occurs **inside of** communication. What I mean by that is, the conversations we have about ourselves and the world around us, actually **become** who we are and the world around us. In other words, your network of conversations becomes reality (your self-and-world view).

Your language contains certain categories or schemas that express your cognitive model of the world. You're not simply using communication to do something or accurately describe something, your conversations **become** something, literally become who you are and create the social and cultural contexts in which you see the world (your background of reality). Language shapes our experience of the environment and ourselves. Words shape perceptions and action, a kind of linguistic relativity theory. For example, if I was in your organization and I wanted to find out about the leadership, I would just ask you "So what's it like to work around here?" And you would give me your "reality" of the organization and its leadership through the network of conversations you had with me. From this perspective, *change is a repetitive process of social construction in which new realities are created, sustained, and modified by the process of communication.* Producing an intentional shift from inauthentic behavior to authentic leadership, then, is a matter of deliberately bringing into existence, through conversations with ourselves and others, a new reality or set of social structures related to **who you are** and **what you are truly committed to.** The transformation or change process actually occurs within and is driven by the communication and conversations you have rather than the reverse.

With respect to authentic leadership, change as an organizational phenomenon necessarily occurs in a context of human social interactions, which form and are formed by communication, i.e., conversations. These interactions produce and reproduce the social structures and actions people know as reality. From this proposition, one could contextualize our work environments as primarily inclusive social networks of language and our leaders as leading these social language networks. Therefore, authentic leadership is not primarily a process that uses communication as a tool, but rather it is more essentially a way of "being" that is created, produced and maintained by and within one's network of conversations.

Where does authentic leadership happen? It happens, between you and another *in the consistent conversations that you engage in*. These conversations create a pattern that become how you choose to function in your day-to-day life. By using thinking and language **deliberately**, a person can intentionally shape his or her background of reality, self-and-world view and ultimately their future. The opportunity is to stop living in the delusion that we are one way in our mind but can speak and act incongruently with that often grandiose and idealized image of ourselves in our head. Ironically from this vantage point, there really is no mystery to why organizations stay stuck in their silos of ineffectiveness. Just like any machine, you are perfectly designed to produce the results you currently produce! The transformation starts to occur when we stop perpetuating the habitual "dead end" thinking and conversations that keep the current "design" in place!

Now this assertion may seem overly simplified to some and it is admittedly very challenging to actually implement given the natural resistance of human beings to change. However, the inherent challenge of sustainably transforming the basically defensive human modus operandi does not make the veracity of the premise stated here any less profound or possible! Be wary of your mind's reaction to diminish this possibility too quickly as trite or overly simplistic. **Your life is what your thoughts and conversations make it!** Don't believe me? Try this test, take the next 24 hours or even just the next 2 hours and notice every single thing that comes out of your mouth and every thought which goes through your head (to the degree that that is humanly possible) and notice if it is "positive and possibility oriented" and forwards what you are "up to" or "negative and overly pessimistic" and provides nothing to move your goals forward. You will be amazed at what you observe! I often joke with my new clients (a bit tongue and cheek because what I am about to say is actually very true), that when you "get" these distinctions I am presenting and actually experience them, you will immediately *EXPONENTIALLY* increase the time available in your schedule because you will stop speaking and thinking about 50% of the things you are currently spending/wasting your time thinking and speaking about which **do not provide anything** toward impacting what you are committed to!

Authentic Leaders Realize They Have A Choice!

Authentic leaders realize and take responsibility for this choice. They "get" that the persistent conversations they have actually *create* their reality rather than merely describe it. The power to transform their world is literally in their conversations. No kidding! Realizing and acting on this concept can be very powerful when you consider that most of the actions that people engage in – in business, in marriage, in parenting – are carried out through conversations. However, most people speak without any intention: they simply say whatever comes to mind. Speak with intention and your actions take on new purpose. Speak with conviction and inspiration and you act with conviction and inspiration.

The current "reality" you say is stopping you is likely to be a conversation or bunch of conversations that you and others are simply in agreement about. To change the reality, one needs to change the conversations that they have convinced themselves are real (like fixed immovable objects of mass and weight). We as human beings made language up but then we forgot that we did that and started to interact with our words as if they were real, fixed, impermeable entities or REALITY. Most organizational problems don't come about because people don't know about their businesses; they come about because people aren't aware of this nuance of the human condition. When we are willing to "give up" for the moment that our conversations are "the truth" and have open, authentic and honest dialogues, former impossibilities start to emerge as possible. In contrast, impasses and inauthentic behaviors abound when we behave like automatons or so called "professionals". To deliver exceptional results in an organization you need to have people who are flexible, who coordinate well and listen well. You need leaders who are passionate about learning how to be authentic and who can promote authenticity throughout their business units.

5

Getting "Present" to How Life Happens

How we typically think life happens....

Linear states in time of the past, present and future, which we inconsequentially talk about and describe as if they happen one after the other and we are just passive bystanders accurately describing them while rarely having much if any direct impact on them.

What actually tends to happens is...

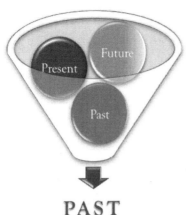

PAST

The past, the future and the present all get collapsed and jumbled up and typically become the past relived in the present, a sort of "self-fulfilling prophecy" for the future. Our "background of reality" filter, that we funnel things through, shapes what we hear and what we see and is largely constructed from the past.

Consider a scenario of speaking with someone at work. You think you are being highly attentive to the conversation, but in actuality you are woefully unaware of the fact that what you are hearing is very different from the words that person is actually saying. They ask you "Where are you with the Jenson project?" and you *hear* "Are you going to be late again (loser) with your analysis of the numbers, because you were late the last time?" Similarly, your boss comes up to you at 4:30 p.m. on that same Friday and asks, "Can you work on Saturday because John can't come in?" You quickly say, "okay" with a forced smile (after all, the last boss you said no to really let you have it") yet as he walks away you proceed to have a litany of derogatory thoughts about him always **"doing"** this to you! How can he even be asking you to work when you have plans to go to the big game with a group of friends and why does this always happen to you?! X#!$@!

When your thoughts are absorbed with **the past**, or with fantasies and anxieties about **the future** because of what has happened in **the past** this pulls you away from what is actually taking place in the **present** thus creating a self-fulfilling prophecy for the future. In these scenarios the self-fulfilling prophecies are 1) anyone who asks me a question doesn't think I am competent; and 2) I can't ever really say no to a request from my boss. Having these beliefs

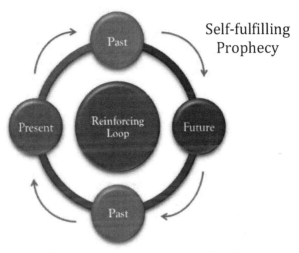

Self-fulfilling Prophecy

and assumptions will continue to perpetuate the frustration from the past into the present and the future. I suggest that in order to understand and alter what is really happening in these conversations one needs to develop a capacity for "Mindful Psychological Presence" or "being present".

Mindful Psychological Presence

Mindful Psychological Presence can be considered an enhanced consciousness of attention to and awareness of current experience or present reality. Most simply said...it is being AWAKE! I have a great interest in the study of consciousness. Unfortunately what I have observed over the years is that the state of consciousness of the typical person at work, or in life in general for that matter, is being only *half* awake. If the person in the scenarios described above was able to develop this capacity for mindful psychological presence, they then could become awake and aware of what is actually being "said" in those conversations. They would notice that they were collapsing the past, present and the future and that the present and future they perceived in the conversations actually was the past relived. Specifically, a core characteristic of mindful psychological presence is *open* or *receptive* awareness and attention, which is reflected in a more regular or sustained consciousness of ongoing events and experience.

Consciousness encompasses the range of both awareness and attention. **Awareness** in general could be said to be the background "radar" of consciousness, continually monitoring the inner and outer environment. One may be aware of stimuli without them being at the center of attention. **Attention** allows us to use our limited active cognitive resources effectively and with rapid execution. Attention is a process of focusing conscious awareness, providing heightened sensitivity to a limited range of experience. In actuality, awareness and attention are intertwined, such that attention continually pulls "figures" out of the "ground" of awareness, holding them focally for varying lengths of time. **Conscious Awareness** allows us to monitor our interactions with the environment, to correlate our past and present experiences and develop a continuity of experience for a feeling of control and ability to plan for future events.

Mindlessness, which is the relative absence of mindful psychological presence, can be defensively motivated, as when an individual refuses to acknowledge or attend to a thought, emotion, motive or object of perception. I have observed that individuals differ in their willingness to be aware and to sustain attention to what is occurring in the present and that this mindful capacity varies within persons, because it can be sharpened or dulled by a variety of factors.

Mindful psychological presence as it relates to authentic leadership is about developing conscious attention to and awareness of how consistent your thinking and conversations are over time and being mindful of whether or not your actions are correlated with the "self" you express yourself to be. It is also largely about being psychologically present to what you are actually saying and subsequently keeping the promises and commitments that you make to others and yourself, in essence "being your word". When one is committed to being an authentic leader, "your word" means something when you make a commitment and at the very least you are responsible for being in communication if you see that you will not fulfill on a commitment you have made no matter how small or inconsequential the commitment may seem. This critically includes having the willingness, regardless of circumstances or excuses, to take accountability for the consequences of not keeping your commitments or "being your word". That is to say, IT MATTERS!

Having said this let me be clear that being an authentic leader does not mean having to be perfect, never making a mistake or never "dropping the ball" and not fulfilling on a commitment. Nor does it mean having to say yes to everything so as to be considered the consummate team player. These global polarities of thought are another by-product of reactionary thinking and being "half-awake" when we do respond to people at work or in life in general. Individuals behaving in this compulsive or automatic way without awareness of or attention to their thinking and behavior are exhibiting a lack of conscious awareness. Being an authentic leader is not about being perfect but rather it is about being psychologically present, awake, and accountable and in communication.

For example going back to our scenarios, if you were psychologically present in the first conversation you would perhaps realize that your colleague asked you, "Where are you with the Jensen project?" and that's it! And if you were psychologically present when your boss asked, "Can you work on Saturday?" You might have realized that a possible reply could have been, "I do understand you're in a bind and while I am truly committed to being a team player, I am also committed to keeping my word and I have made other commitments I choose not to break. So I will not be able to come in on Saturday. However, I am more than willing to support the team at another time."

Now you may be saying, well that's just "crazy" talk or ridiculously unreasonable! First of all, you say, "I know what my co-worker *really* meant when he asked the question about the Jenson project and furthermore I could NEVER say that to my boss, people just can't do that in the "<u>real world!</u>" To that I say...you are right...it is unreasonable...but that doesn't mean it can't be done or that I haven't seen it effectively done by others, including myself. No one ever said authentic leadership was reasonable or for that matter easy, worthwhile endeavors rarely are. If it were easy everyone would be engaging in it, right? Although it <u>can be</u> *easier* if you are consistent with keeping your commitments and being your word. When you start to operate in this way people start to realize that you are someone who honors your commitments, that you are not to be manipulated and that you mean what you say. That is, your word means something to you no matter who you make your commitments to - your boss, your family or a friend.

Mindful psychological presence captures a quality of consciousness that is characterized by clarity and vividness of current experience and functioning and thus stands in contrast to the mindless, less "awake" states of habitual or automatic functioning that may be chronic for many individuals. Adding clarity and vividness to experience, mindful psychological presence or "being present", also seems to contribute to well-being and happiness in a direct way. For example, mindful psychological presence may be important in disengaging individuals from automatic thoughts, habits and unhealthy behavior patterns and subsequently could play a key role in fostering informed and self-endorsed behavioral regulation, which has long been associated with well-being enhancement. In addition, it is entirely conceivable that once you start to operate with mindful psychological presence you will be the recipient of less stress when faced with the sort of situations mentioned as well as a myriad of others. For instance, when someone approaches you with what you have perceived in the past as a "confronting" and stressful scenario, now you can peacefully stop, get psychologically present, listen, choose, and respond. In these pivotal moments, having a developed and psychologically present compelling personal purpose accompanied by a strong sense of self creates a background of reality that dramatically increases your probability for success.

6

Deconstructing Reality
Is vs. Seems

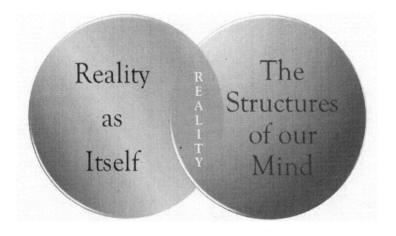

Let's move into the experiential reality of your life related to this idea of mindful psychological presence. What is a process of thinking which you can put into place to continuously examine and realize how your thoughts are manifesting themselves as your world? When we don't engage in mindful psychological presence and simply react to a world that we believe "is" out there stopping us from being authentic...we don't realize that our "reality" is **only a version** of how life "seems" to us. You see, we can never describe reality as itself. We can only describe reality as it is to us, which is a synthesis of reality plus our own personal mental models. Consider watching a democrat and a republican attempt to talk about the same problematic issue on television. More often than not, each person comes up with a totally antithetical and vehemently defended conclusion about the source of the problem from which that issue has emerged.

Too often we are so focused on being "right" about the way that things are *to us* that we don't realize that we are stuck due to our insistence that our reality is clearly the "right" one. That is to say, as much as you may want to convince yourself or others that the boss is doing something *to you*, or your coworker really *is a jerk*, it actually only "seems" that way to you. It is not that it "is" that way. The "what happened" of the situations were, something was said, the structures in your mind from the past made it mean something *other than* what was said and that became what you heard and your reality in the present.

It's so difficult to separate ourselves from our perspective that even if our perspective does change we may be inclined to feel that it is the world rather than *our way of looking at the world* that has changed. Check out the visual example on the left of this paragraph. What is it a picture of? Is it of an old woman or of a young woman with a feather in her hat? It's both, depending on your perspective. Not only does the world *affect* our perception but also the world we experience is actually *formed by* our perception. In other words, our perception is reciprocal with the world we experience. Perception both affects and is affected by the world as we experience it. We do not perceive simply in terms of what is "out there in the world". Our expectations and beliefs largely **determine** what is "out-there in the world!"

Much of what goes on under the banner of leadership development amounts to helping people develop more skills or capacities to cope, but cope within the design of their current self-and-world view. The authentic leadership development approach proposed in these pages takes up a point of view *outside* the "world" of this current assumptive design, so that we can actually look at the very principles by which our view is shaped. Elucidating the taken for granted realities of everyday life in a group or organization can become a force for understanding and transformation, and establishing a new reality based on the kind of every day environment desired by leaders committed to authenticity.

7

Life as a Constructed Narrative

So if we can see life or "reality" as an occurrence, which "seems" a particular way to us as opposed to being a fixed reality, which "is" a particular way, we could more accurately start **creating** life as a constructed narrative. Which is actually what we are already doing, we just don't realize it. To be a person is to have a story to tell. The answer to the question "Can I really make a difference?" is often organized in the form of a life narrative, i.e., a story about why you believe you can or can't related to who you are and why your life is where it is right now. Personal narratives are the story of a person's constructed self and represent an internal structure for considering, "who I was, who I am (and why), and who I might become." Identity is merely a story created, told, revised, and retold throughout life. We know or discover ourselves, and reveal ourselves to others, by the narratives we share about ourselves. Often people have adjustment difficulties to life when the story of their life, as created by them or others, does not match their lived experience.

Highly developed self-knowledge in terms of a life story provides the authentic leader with a strong sense of self because it organizes life events into a coherent unfolding process that establishes connections between events so that a person's life is experienced in a fluid and comprehensible way. The language of a person's life story provides the authentic leader with a "meaning system", from which to feel, think, and act as well as revise and redirect when necessary. It enables him or her to analyze and interpret reality in a way that gives it a personal meaning. Life narratives provide authentic leaders with a self that can be expressed through the leadership role. Your passion for what you are interested in impacting in this life grows from the foundation of values that have been formed by your life experience. These values are essential to the individual and are highly personalized, not because they are socially acceptable, as in they look good in a mission or purpose statement, but because you have actually experienced them to be true. In fact, positive and negative events in a person's life can trigger deep change in their values and consequently their sense of self.

Every idea you hold passionately has a background in your personal experience. As an example, Dr. Rollo May the foremost spokesperson for existential psychology in the United States, grew up in in the early 1900's surrounded by a virtually non-existent intellectual climate. In fact, when his older sister had a psychotic breakdown, May's father was convinced that too much education was the root cause of the illness. Not being emotionally close to his parents, who had a very contentious relationship and ultimately separated, May lived a particularly isolated childhood. During his youth he acquired an interest in art and literature and in early adulthood he received a bachelor's degree in teaching. However, by his second year of pouring himself into his work as a teacher, May found that the harder he worked the less effective he became. Finally, in the spring of his second year he had a nervous breakdown. He had come to the realization that the rules, values and principles that he had used to guide his life up to that point did not work for him anymore. It is from this point that May began to listen to his inner voice. Later upon reflection, He concluded that this total collapse of his former way of being in life was what allowed for his inner voice to be heard.

As a result, May entered Union Theological Seminary in New York in 1933 to inquire into the nature of human beings. It is there that he met the well know existential theologian and philosopher Paul Tillich, a refugee from Germany and a faculty member at the seminary. The exchange of ideas through this friendship forged much of May's philosophy. He was ordained as a minister and served as a pastor for 2 years, however, found the work less than fulfilling. He then went on to earn a PhD in clinical psychology at the relatively advanced age of 40. Important to note is that prior to receiving his doctorate May went through the most profound experience of his life. He contracted tuberculosis and spent 3 years in the hospital. At that time, no medication for tuberculosis was available and May did not know whether he would live or die. He felt totally helpless for a while but after a time started to develop insights into the nature of his illness. He noticed that patients around him who accepted their illness were the ones who tended to die. In contrast, those who fought their condition tended to survive. He decided to be personally responsible for fighting his disease and for asserting his own will to live. May discovered that the sick individual, either physiologically or psychologically, must be an active participant in the recovery process. He determined that people could aspire to psychological and physiological health only through confronting the unconscious core of their existence. After May recovered from his illness he wrote his dissertation on the subject of anxiety. May went on to write numerous best selling books and attain prestigious scientific and professional awards in psychology, ultimately becoming the best-known American representative of the existential psychological movement.

Throughout this example, one can see that Rollo May's personal experiences certainly shaped and were shaped by his unique desires, values and ultimate life narrative. He had innumerable opportunities to construct a different narrative given the extraordinary obstacles he faced at any given time. He chose to construct the narrative, which became for him a fulfilling life. What is your constructed narrative? Is your experience of leadership or your job or your life for that matter something you have to "deal" with, something you are acting as if you are a "victim of", perhaps a constant siege of fatiguing fires you have to put out everyday? Or does it occur as an opportunity to make a difference, to fulfill on your life's passions, to contribute and be contributed to?

8

Self as a Narrative Project
Discovering and Creating Your Authentic Self

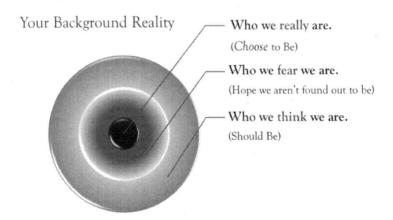

Your Background Reality

— **Who we really are.**
(*Choose* to Be)

— **Who we fear we are.**
(Hope we aren't found out to be)

— **Who we think we are.**
(Should Be)

The existential philosophers thought of "self" as a narrative project and in many ways it truly is. How we normally operate inside of this "project" is we **act** like the person **we think we should be** and for a while we may even think **that is who we are.** This is motivated by our need to hide **who we fear we are** because if people really knew how "messed up" we were they surely wouldn't work with us!

Then way deep down in the belly of our being is this rich deep pool of light trying to shine through of **who we really are**. If you are upset with the current game that you've got going, create a new one. For example, if you hear yourself saying: "I wish I could do things differently", "I wish I had the money to do what I really want to do", "Why won't they listen to me?" "I'm too set in my ways to change now", "I don't have the time", "I can't afford it", "It sounds too risky", "What if I fail?"....

You'll find that you'll create other conversations when you come alive while discovering and creating your authentic self. One of them is that you get to experience your emotions again. Remember fun, excitement, anticipation?!! Those long lost emotions that were trapped in sublimation or fear, those that you suppressed when you didn't want to expose the real you. Those you kept to yourself when you felt they weren't acceptable for an adult to show in the "professional" world. You will experience energy that seems boundless and it will be coming from the knowledge that you created the whole thing called your life! That you are responsible for it, and you accept it for what it is currently. Note here, I said, "accept it" for what it is currently not "settle for it". You'll know that the future will be totally ok, because you will be responsible for it and create it. If you consider and actually act on the concepts I have shared with you so far, you will find that when you become willing to simply put **your authentic self fully out there** for others to be with, that you will experience true self-expression. Forget the fear that you've always had about being right about **what** you express. Just tell the truth, without resentment or malice, with a commitment to fulfilling on your purpose and see what happens. Communicate totally for once in your life. What aim is there in holding back?

Track II

The Practical Application of ALD

9

Becoming an Authentic Leader

More than just positive thinking...

Business as Usual vs. *Breakthrough*

The practicality of becoming an authentic leader lies inside of one's commitment to moving from "business as usual" ways of operating to what I call "breakthrough". A breakthrough is an extraordinary and unpredictable outcome. I have experienced and observed that authentic leaders develop their sense of self and their self-and-world views through deliberately committing to and implementing Breakthrough Projects. Why? Accomplishing a breakthrough project requires a leader and his/her team to interact in a specific fashion, which generates an interruption in business as usual forms of operating. Breakthrough projects challenge traditional wisdom regarding what can and cannot be accomplished according to the current conversations in a group or in an organization as a whole. A breakthrough project acts as a paradoxical learning laboratory in that to fulfill on a breakthrough project one must provide authenticity in leadership, something the person in the leadership role *does not know how to do yet*, however, it is in the commitment to the accomplishment of the breakthrough result that the project becomes the vehicle for developing that authenticity in leadership. This is where the personal point of view of the leader is developed through personal experience, personal learning and personal reflection while executing the breakthrough project.

First let's distinguish producing "breakthrough" results from other forms of business results. Referencing the diagram on the following page, a "business as usual" result, is some outcome that is predicable, which you have done before and predictably can do again. A "stress goal" is the next level of result typically produced in an organization and what most people perceive as "performing at a high level". This level of operating tends to create and perpetuate "burnout" because the stress goal team does exactly what the business as usual team does; they just do it with more intensity, at a quicker pace, and through longer hours until they finally achieve a forced outcome. Then everyone breathes a collective sigh of relief, "bloodied and bruised", cynically discussing the absurdity of having to continually operate in ineffective "fire drill" mode in these instances, rolls their eyes, shrugs their shoulders and goes back to business as usual (until next time, of course!).

A breakthrough, in comparison, is an entirely unpredictable outcome. In fact, those who are **not**

Stress Goal

Business as Usual

committed to anything changing will try to dismiss the breakthrough goal as unrealistic, unattainable and perhaps irresponsible to even consider and will spend their time having conversations defending that point of view which is based in the past. They resist the logic that the breakthrough outcome needs to go beyond the current limitations of what you know how to do so that a shift can take place in **who you are being** in order to accomplish it. Remember, you are perfectly designed to produce the results you currently have. In order to produce different results, it stands to reason that one would need to discover something new that "they don't know that they don't know" about themselves, about others and about the situation. To this the naysayers will placate to your fear and say the project is unreasonable and can never be accomplished.

Actually, on a certain level they are right, it *can never* be accomplished doing what they and you currently know how to do. The reason being that breakthrough results cannot come from business as usual, known ways of operating! Authentic leaders have to grapple with **who they need to *be and become*** in order to organize themselves and others in a way that intentionally advances performance beyond what can reasonably be expected based on past experience. Without a commitment in time for a breakthrough result *the person currently does not know how to fulfill on,* everything I have presented so far becomes merely academic and more positive thinking jargon. When you stay conceptual and abstract, i.e., talking about these notions and principles rather than using them, there is no actual "skin in the game" and no authentic leadership or breakthrough results.

One of the central variables in becoming an authentic leader is developing one's tenacity in making and keeping commitments. Many people in leadership positions "commit" or more accurately "agree" to goals that they have no intention of "owning". That way, if it looks like they might not achieve the goal they simply move it back instead of having a breakthrough in their leadership toward producing the goal for the original target date they "committed" to (after all, no big deal, it never really was *their* goal anyway). It is this "owning of one's reality" by honoring one's commitments and embracing the inherent struggle with how to keep those commitments that separates authentic leaders from others simply "occupying" leadership positions. The breakthrough result is unreasonable and cannot occur unless transformation in authentic leadership and ownership takes place. You ultimately "own" your commitments for your sake, not anyone else, because owning them has integrity and having integrity with your word correlates with being an authentic leader.

In order to operate at this level of breakthrough one has to operate differently, be differently, do things differently. It is uncomfortable because **the nature of a breakthrough is that you don't know how to cause it *but* you are committed to it.** A business as usual project design starts from today and looks at all the things you need to *become first before* you can *behave* differently to finally *be* what or who you ultimately aspire to be. For example, let's say you aspire to be the number one business unit in your organization related to revenue generation. The business as usual way of designing this project would be, you start out with the conversation that, "Once you become a business unit which has a budget big enough to support adding the resources for the execution of such a lofty goal,

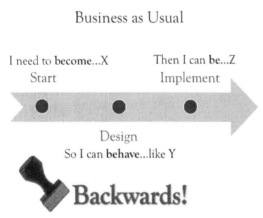

Business as Usual

I need to become...X   Then I can be...Z
Start   Implement

Design
So I can behave...like Y

Backwards!

then, you can behave in a way that can attain that goal and ultimately be the number one revenue generating business unit in your organization!" Sounds reasonable, right? Well, if you are interested in producing breakthroughs, this approach is actually BACKWARDS! It's like saying, "I really am committed to being an authentic leader!" and "Once I *become* the VP of my division, I can then *behave* authentically (because I will have the power to do so) and can finally *be* the authentic leader I am in my head!"

Conversely, with a breakthrough objective, you stand in the future, and picture yourself six months, maybe a year from now, maybe longer and you <u>say</u> what the target will be and then you go back to the beginning and you create a likely scenario of how you got there, as if YOU ARE THERE, NOW! You actually <u>plan backwards</u> from the results <u>already achieved</u> asking what would have had to happen at each point along the way to overcome any obstacles and to have met your objective.

BREAKTHROUGH

Behave as they do...

Become what they are!

Be that person NOW!

Design from "That Future is Fulfilled!"

STAND FOR A FUTURE!

I have a client who after hearing this concept threw his arms up in amazement and exclaimed, "Oh my gosh! I get it!" as if he had actually seen something in his mind's eye. Well he had, and proceeded to share with me a personal experience to which he could immediately relate this concept. He said that he had always wanted to climb a particular mountain range and he had planned for it for years. Reading everything he could about the range and mountain climbing techniques in general, he had also visited the base of the mountain many times before, looking up the mountainside at the challenge of reaching the apex. Then one day he was perusing the Internet and found some pictures of an expedition of climbers who had conquered that particular mountain and had posted pictures from the top of the mountain, their journey accomplished, looking back down at how they got there. When he looked at the pictures of their journey's triumph down to the bottom of the mountain, he immediately <u>saw himself there</u> at the apex (what he would be wearing, how he would be feeling, the warmth of the sun on his face, the sense of accomplishment he would have, etc.) and in turn had a flood of ideas come to mind which he had not even thought of before, regarding how to tactically accomplish this dream. In other words, it wasn't until he looked from actually **being there, standing in** the accomplishment of his journey completed, "owning it", *no kidding*, that he could see things which were blind to him while looking at his goal as someone trying to become something first in order to "get there". From this insight he realized he was living in "someday" he would climb the mountain rather than he is a mountain climber now, the mountain has been conquered and all that is standing between him and the apex is space and time. So, <u>HE COMMITTED TO A DATE</u> and fulfilled on his dream. It's a subtle distinction, but tremendously powerful! Authentic leaders commit to breakthrough projects so that they can **be the leader they are committed to being NOW!** They then gravitate towards behaving as that person behaves (because it is "REAL" now) and become who and what that person becomes. You don't "wait" for the "right" situation, position of authority, enough money, training, or perfect job to start being an authentic leader. It's standing in the

ACCOMPLISHED FUTURE NOW and making a commitment in time to fulfill on that future which causes things to "miraculously" move forward.

When people vehemently resist committing to clearly articulated breakthrough outcomes (heaven forbid they set themselves up to "look bad") they would be better served not occupying a leadership position. For them leadership is conceptual, not WHO they are. They are in actuality more interested in doing the work of a manager of tasks, which is a very valid and essential position in an organization but is distinct from what it takes to be a leader of people and of breakthrough results. This doesn't preclude leaders from having or needing the competencies of effective management, they just aren't held hostage by systems, processes and protocols from the past. On the other hand, I've met those who want to talk all day long about how visionary they are and what a "people person" they are, thinking that is primarily the "work" of leadership, but who are sorely lacking strategic judgment, the ability to guide the management and implementation of a project plan and any semblance of an organized existence system to track and cause their commitments. This extreme polarity isn't leadership either. To accomplish authentic leadership one must be committed to the mastery of this management and leadership paradox.

10

Insight Learning

Anxiety Exciting!

FULFILLING Messy

Becoming an authentic leader is experiential! The concepts and process of authentic leadership development outlined in this book are aimed at discovery! It is about mastering insight learning. It is not about waiting until you know enough, then you will start being authentic. This is about experiential development and insight learning through experience! In other words, learning how to be an authentic leader and produce breakthrough results by grappling with **being an authentic leader** and **committing**

to and producing breakthrough results. Expect some anxiety, it's messy; and it's also exciting and fulfilling. I find most individual's lives, when you pull back the curtain, are somewhat messy and anxiety ridden already, I'm just adding the exciting and fulfilling part!

Truly though, taking this sort of development on is about seriously making a commitment to being in a persistent, consistent, passionate, inquiry regarding what it means to be an authentic leader and how you are going to be that and fulfill on that in your day-to-day accountabilities. That may sound straight forward enough, however, there is a big difference between **wanting** something and **being committed** to it. If you are ever interested to know what people are really committed to, look in two places...their calendars and their checkbooks!! Whatever they are spending their money on and have scheduled in their calendars **is what they are truly committed to**. Period! Everything else is just a "good idea", something fun or interesting to talk about and pretend they are committed to.

Don't be fooled by intelligently crafted rhetoric waxing on about how they (not you of course!) "... really *are* committed to being an authentic leader" if you notice that becoming one doesn't involve these two criteria. I have heard championship coaches from numerous sports address this inconsistent nature of the average person's commitments by noting that, "Everybody wants to be on a championship team, but it's the rare individual who wants to come to practice!" In the business world this shows up as, everyone wants to have authenticity and amazing performance in their organizational cultures, but few are willing to take the risks to lead that transformation.

There are two typical models of insight learning situations. The first model involves what might be called short-circuiting. An example of this is when a long and tedious way of executing some familiar task suddenly is seen from a quick and expedient way of doing it. Once this has come about it is so obvious that everyone agrees, "Of course, why didn't we think of that before?" It is like driving to work by a long, roundabout route and suddenly you realize that if you go through a side street you can cut fifteen minutes off of your commute. The second model is the heuristic effect. The word heuristic comes from the Greek word *hueriskein*, meaning to discover or to find. It is synonymous with the word *eureka*, the "aha" moment! For example, a problem has been impossible to solve, then suddenly in a flash of insight and without any additional information the solution becomes clear. It's all a matter of the first attention area. A flash of insight comes about simply by looking at one area of the problem before another. A very slight shift in attention can make all the difference.

The insight is due to a change of the entry point in a sequence; therefore one can deliberately increase the possibility of insight solutions by changing the entry point in any sequence of thoughts or events. This would be done by attention not to the problem itself but to the context or precursors of the problem. It could also be done by deliberately starting attention at different points, or even by random disrupting stimuli from outside. For example, as a consultant my mere presence in meetings with a group in an organization causes a disruption in the typical pattern the group would normally operate in. This simple type of disrupting intervention could be enough to cause insight for a group, which is stuck in a particular debilitating pattern of operating.

So what primarily stops insight learning?

Having to be Right and Making Others Wrong!

Congruent with the concept, "It is darkest before the dawn", so it is right before a breakthrough. In fact it can be so uncomfortable that right before the insight leading to a breakthrough might occur, many people stop and retreat back to what they know so that they can be right and protect their egos! Take a moment and look at your life. Visualize some situation where you know you have been right, and it was very reasonable to you that you were right, but where you didn't get what you wanted. I just had a situation where an executive I was coaching was complaining about her boss and gave me  a list of reasons why she was right about her complaints. I asked her how long she had had these complaints that she was right about and she stopped, reflected, smirked and said for 15 years! As her defense she noted "trying" a few times to change the bosses perception with no success so it was really unreasonable, if she wanted to keep her job, to continue to try doing anything about it. Yet she was clearly miserable in many regards and was reserving the right to stay in the situation while covertly (and overtly at times) continuing for 15 years to make her boss wrong!

I want you to get the idea that the world you live in is not a reasonable place to be. In fact, very little about it is reasonable. So if you are running your life in a reasonable fashion, the safest assumption to make is that _YOU ARE NOT GOING TO GET WHAT YOU WANT VERY OFTEN!_ And there is a logical explanation for that, it is: reasonableness equals rightness. To be there in living your life, literally means you could end up losing every scenario you set up and the only thing you get out of your stories is knowing how "right" you are! And the people you call your friends gather around you while you describe your clearly "irreconcilable" situation (acting as if you are forced to stay there), you get them to agree with you that you are right, then to alleviate the discomfort they shove a drink in your hand! Wooohoo! You didn't get what you were after, and you are still frustrated the next day. How's that workin' for ya? *What else stops insight learning?*

Hearing but not Listening

Did you know that if you presented a rat with 3 tunnels, only one of which has cheese in it, the rat would explore all the possible options available to run through until he finds the cheese? And, after reinforcement, he will disregard the tunnels with no cheese, and go down only the one with the sought after prize. Conversely, if you take away the cheese he will soon learn that it's gone, and will begin to explore all other options again, looking for the reward. Human beings, in stark contrast, will go up a tunnel looking for whatever the "cheese" of the situation is, never get any, but will continue to go up the same tunnel for a life time. What is  driving them? Reasonableness and rightness by hearing but not listening! That is, they say to themselves: "I know I saw cheese go up this tunnel. I know I can find it again #X$!@%*$!"

So they spend a lifetime without the cheese they desperately seek, however, always being able to explain to anyone who will listen, that they are up a very reasonable tunnel and that the cheese SHOULD be up that tunnel! One of my favorite examples of this is the justification I hear people use for continuing to stay in an organization, which they complain about as having a dysfunctional inauthentic culture. They don't understand why "*their leadership*" is so inauthentic yet they themselves choose not to take a stand for an alteration of the current suppressive ineffective culture by engaging in authentic leadership development for themselves. Not having any intention of leaving, they continue to complacently stay in the dysfunction, blaming everyone else and justifying their apathetic performance and resignation by stating that, "Well, it's this way anywhere you go!"

When you are not listening to the perpetual onslaught of complaints which are coming out of **your mouth** at nausea or you are reserving the right to listen through filters such as "this is just the way it is", I'm right/their wrong, good/bad, us/them, should/must, it's not my fault, whose to blame, something's wrong here, and choosing not to be responsible for **your part** in these sorts of conversations as well as in the perpetuation of the whole mess, insight learning and providing any semblance of authentic leadership will be a distant dream.

Believing there is a World "Out-There"

The third condition which stops insight learning is believing there is a world "out-there" stopping you from getting what you want out of life. Just think about the incredible number of people who spend their entire lifetime being "right" and very "reasonable" about the "world out-there" administering them an "unfair" deal. They never get to a state of sustainable peace; they just get to complain about

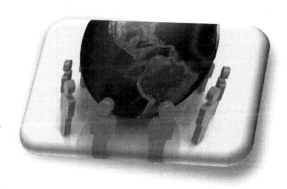

everything that isn't fair about the world. Endlessly! They never face up to the truth of the matter, which is that they aren't getting the results they want, _and they don't address that!_ Instead they spend their lives talking about all the reasons why they should be acknowledged for being right about why they can't get the results that they want!

It seems to come down to a willingness to distinguish what our "Self-and-World View" is. If you're running your life up a tunnel (or a series of them) with no "cheese" for you...in other words you can literally hear yourself saying the same complaints over and over and over again as if they are a "fixed reality", i.e., world out-there that you have nothing to do with and that is somehow stopping you, you are losing the games that **you** are setting up for yourself! Yet you forgot one very important principle, **you** set them up through your self-and-world view and the choices you have made up to this point. The good news about that is, if **you** set them up, **you** can also stop playing them and set up other games for yourself in which you can win, feel accomplished and have fun doing it! Simply go to work on altering your self-and-world view and implementing the other key concepts as noted in these pages.

How Shall I Live My Life?

That brings us back to the beginning. Having the courage to answer the fundamental question... "How shall I live my life?" Authenticity in leadership at this point in our society is the road less travelled. And, as you may have gather through your journey in reading this book and perhaps your own leadership journey, this road is not for the faint of heart. It is for those who want to learn how to conquer fear and anxiety rather than merely survive it. And to learn to be responsible for the fact that rarely does anyone ever do anything to us, we do it to ourselves by the choices we make and putting off responsibility for the future onto someone else or some organization seemingly outside of ourselves.

Authentic Leadership is about Generating Breakthroughs in Reasonableness

The reasonable man adapts himself to the world; the unreasonable man adapts the world to himself. All progress depends on the unreasonable man.

George Bernard Shaw

By observation, I conclude that people who have to be "reasonable" have to be "right", spending most of their time *complaining and explaining* why they can't be the authentic leader they truly want to be and by default are putting on an *act* every single day. This I believe accounts for the massive fear, resignation, fatigue and apathy we see in a majority of people in our organizations today. In fact, research has shown that "burn out" in people in organizations is very often directly related to the energy expended in being inauthentic and suppressing authentic behavior rather than being "over worked". I'm not saying that if you become an authentic leader you will never have a bad day, or not be tired, or even not lose your job. But I am saying that it won't be that devastating if you do because you will know who you are, you will be clear about what you are committed to and you will just go create that somewhere else. You will not be living in fear or reaction to a world "out-there" holding you hostage by despair and anxiety-ridden thoughts of what may happen to you.

When you develop yourself in becoming an authentic leader you find out and create who you really are and where you really want to go and you won't spend your energy rowing upstream in the river of being right. When you are tired it is a peaceful exhaustion of accomplishment. Then life consists of rising every morning, getting psychologically present, taking your body onto the river of "your authentic life", dropping onto a boogie board with no paddles, and just riding along with the natural current of your own true self expression.

The medium for breaking through reasonableness and rightness is language or conversation, which is generated from your thinking. Speaking is a reflection of your thinking. Conversation is the medium of producing results in business and in life in general. Conversations include – thinking, speaking and listening, reading & writing. Becoming an authentic leader and being authentic doesn't "just happen". It takes commitment over time, responsibility for your thinking and conversations, and consistent actions in line with your thinking and speaking.

11

Authentically Leading
Breakthrough Projects

Organizing for Advancing Beyond
"Business as Usual"

Principles

Authentic Commitment
to Results

Breakthroughs Originate
from "Presenting
Problems"

Communication
Framework for Action

The ABC Principles

A breakthrough project is the outcome of an **Authentic commitment to a result** that is beyond what is predictable. Results are *predictable* when historical data exist to support the notion that the results can be produced.

Breakthroughs originate from "presenting problems". A "problem" is initially heard as something bad or wrong. Something that shouldn't be! Here I call problems - **"presenting problems"** and they are actually the only access and gateway to breakthroughs. In fact, breakthroughs originate *from* "presenting problems". **NO PRESENTING PROBLEMS, NO BREAKTHROUGHS.** Therefore a presenting problem takes on a very different meaning.

A breakthrough project has a uniquely distinct **Communication framework that evokes clear actions**. The conscious design and use of such a framework is critical for the authentic leader's success in effectively leading and subsequently causing a breakthrough in performance.

The next set of pages will go into more depth and detail expanding these three key fundamental ABC principles of organizing oneself and others to advance beyond "business as usual". Following which is a structural outline of the basic components of a breakthrough project.

Defining A "Presenting Problem"

A "presenting problem" is a demand for action outside of one's automatic response. Why do I call it a "presenting problem"? Because it is a person or group's "perception" of a situation that "presents" itself or is "seen" initially as a problem, i.e., something that "shouldn't be" or something you have to "deal with" and it is "bad" that it has happened.

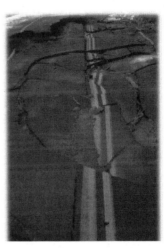

○ Presenting Problem: Circumstances fall short of one's commitment.

○ Presenting Problems occur in the gap between a committed result and the predictable outcome.

○ Breakthroughs arise predictably out of "Presenting Problems".

Presenting problems are typically reacted to in this negative way. I am proposing that in actuality they can be observed as an opportunity, which could cause you to shift attention and see things differently (remember, insight learning is due to a change of the entry point in a sequence). This perceptual change, sparked by needing to resolve the presenting problem, is often the opening that lets you see opportunities for previously unconsidered actions.

As an example, consider the common situation in which initial cost estimates for a project, say constructing a building, turn out to have been far too low. To avoid this situation, many organizations inflate early estimates to create "padding" for unplanned mistakes. This padding can take the form of additional resources, time buffers, extra money allocation and so on. Then if the original estimate is exceeded, but still within the "padding" amount, no "presenting problem" occurs and no "out of the ordinary" action is required. In an organization that commits to schedules and budgets without additional "padding", this same situation would be a "presenting problem". The productivity implications could be enormous and are usually seen during economic down times when companies are charged with doing more with less and often surprisingly tend to outperform during these "down turns". In other words, during economic downtimes organizations can't afford to put "padding in" so people are "forced" to deal with presenting problems and have breakthroughs in their thinking and being.

As seen through this example, it is apparent why being an authentic leader is a must in order to fulfill on breakthrough accomplishments. Authentic leaders do not reserve the right to hedge bets driven by the need to falsely look good! In "business as usual" organizations, presenting problems are typically seen as bad and to be avoided at all costs (which in actuality causes people to "cover things up" and "hide" what is really going on, usually to the company's detriment), however, in their most powerful form "presenting problems" can go well beyond the usual sense of the word "problem" and provide an opening for amazing and extraordinary action!

Declaring a "Presenting Problem"

The typical human reaction when initially faced with a problem is to not address it early on, acknowledge it with co-workers one feels "safe" with but not addressing it directly at its source, wait and see what happens and/or "hope" it works itself out. Until there is a compelling authentic commitment that causes a situation to be experienced as a

○ Resolution must be a departure from the past, unprecedented and extraordinary.

○ A specific methodology to resolving presenting problems as opportunities.

○ The bigger the gap, the bigger the presenting problem, the more expansive the breakthrough.

"presenting problem" which stands in the way of the fulfillment of that authentic commitment, effective actions will not be taken to "declare" the situation as a clearly defined "presenting problem". The fundamental principle is that there are no "presenting problems" independent of authentic commitments. A leader, a group of leaders or a project team cannot clearly declare a "presenting problem" if there is no authentic commitment that causes the situation to occur as a "presenting problem".

So what tends to happen is people simply revert to commiserating and complaining in the halls and in their respective offices about the problem that no one is willing to publicly address by declaring it as a "presenting problem" in a committed way to resolving it without making people wrong. What is missing is an authentic commitment that allows the "presenting problem" to occur as an opportunity for a breakthrough in this "business as usual" way of ineffective operating.

A great example of this is a manufacturing client of mine whose management saw employee performance issues related to operator ineffectiveness as a critical problem causing the recently missed quarterly results in their business. After some investigational interviews of my own, however, I found out that the employees did not share this point of view. For them there was no critical problem related to lack of operator effectiveness at all, rather, they saw a number of **different** critical problems that **needed** to be addressed (but hadn't been outside of the usual complaints around the water cooler) such as an uncaring and ineffective management group, unfair compensation policies and unrealistic performance metrics. You can imagine the organization's dilemma.

This example illustrates that until there is an authentic commitment that causes a situation to be experienced as a "presenting problem" for all, no "presenting problem" will be declared and effective actions will not be taken. The same situation, missing the quarterly numbers, appeared differently for the managers than for the project teams because of their seemingly differing commitments. As soon as they were unequivocally aligned on both sets of commitments having equal importance, the employees' commitments and upper level management's commitments becoming one set of jointly owned authentic commitments, then both scenarios became equally important "presenting problems" which could then be declared by both parties, and appropriate creative action followed.

Characteristics of Authentic Commitment

There is a correlation between the magnitude of a breakthrough and the size of gap between "business as usual" results and the new level of results committed to: the bigger the commitment, the bigger the "presenting problems" and also the bigger the potential breakthrough. A small commitment will provide little or no possibility of "presenting problems" offering opportunities for breakthroughs. Therefore, minor "presenting problems" rarely demand sufficient action and energy to effect breakthroughs. Obviously, commitments to aggressive goals with the potential for large "presenting problems" have high risk associated with them. That's part of any game worth playing and unfortunately, breakthrough results cannot be achieved by playing the game safe.

○ The bigger the commitment the bigger the breakthrough

○ Commitment is definitive and without strings

○ The commitment is possible only when chosen freely

○ A breakthrough project is the result of an *authentic* commitment to a result that is <u>beyond</u> what is *predictable.*

Commitment is always absolute and without strings attached. This implies that commitment is made for no reason. A commitment tied to a particular reason is "qualified" because if the reason goes away or is invalidated then the commitment will disappear. Clearly, people consider reasons before making commitments, but once the commitment is made, fulfillment of it cannot be contingent on the reason. In addition, commitment is possible only when people are given a choice. If a person isn't given the freedom to say "no," then his or her "yes" has little to no power. When formulating breakthrough projects, people are often asked what stipulations, if any, their commitments have. Each person is given the choice to construct his or her personal commitment and through this process, the group commitment is constructed for the overall project.

I've tested the validity of this framework while working in my consulting firm with small, and newer companies (my own included). These types of companies typically have amazing breakthroughs in performance. Why? First of all, smaller and new, start-up companies have natural pressures to commit to achieving extraordinary results. If they promise ordinary results, what is the motivation to do business with them? Once promises for extraordinary results are made and the inevitable "presenting problems" occur, the small company environment supports the possibility of a breakthrough because changing the commitment, extending the schedule, throwing in more people, writing off the project are typically not options for a small or new company. Therefore, having a breakthrough becomes the only viable alternative. They are literally "boxed into it". This is the magic! In practice, the strength of small companies faced with a myriad of "presenting problems" is actually their *lack* of flexibility rather than any additional degrees of freedom. Therefore, a breakthrough project is designed specifically to apply pressure during a compressed time frame so as to "force" the issue of truly transforming one's way of "being" while grappling with how to produce a breakthrough result.

A Framework for Communication as Action

To have conversations which forward the clarity of people's commitments could be said to be the essence of an authentic leader's job. This requires developing a well-defined framework for being in clear communication that causes action. As previously stated, most people speak very unintentionally. The ambiguity caused by this unintentional way of speaking tends to generate frustration and ineffectiveness between the parties engaged in these dialogues. For this reason, developing clarity of what is actually being said, not said and committed to in a conversation is a critical shift, which needs to take place for authentic leaders and their teams to be effective. One of the biggest deterrents to effectiveness in communication is when people think they are engaging in the same conversational dialogue, when in fact they are in 2, 3, or 4+ different dialogues at the same time bouncing from one focus to another with no clear intent as to the purpose or outcome desired from the conversation as a whole.

It is no wonder that most meetings end up going around in incoherent circles with participants having a very convoluted understanding of what actually is getting accomplished (if anything) and who is going to be accountable for moving what forward. In order to effectively execute breakthrough projects, I have found that groups need to become clear about what conversation they are in at any given moment in order to manage the "fog" that tends to emerge when people start talking to one another. I suggest accomplishing this through "Seven Intentional Authentic Dialogues".

- Seven Intentional Authentic Dialogues
  - Authentic Relating
  - Invention & Exploration
  - Choosing Options
  - Facts & Figures
  - Action & Accountability
  - Presenting Problems
  - Acknowledgement

I have distinguished seven dialogues, which I consider critical to manage in your meetings and conversations in general, especially for the effective design and implementation of a breakthrough project. They are: Relating through authentic purpose, Invention and exploration, Choosing options, Facts and figures, Action and accountability, Presenting problems: Preempting/managing and resolving, and Acknowledgement, accomplishment and completion. By managing the direction of the conversation as a whole and distinguishing what dialogue the group is in at any given time, people can think together more effectively and with greater alacrity and purpose. The authentic leader needs to be aware of whether the conversation as a whole in a meeting is getting collapsed into multiple dialogues at the same time and/or what dialogue may be missing if the conversation goes off track. Managing what conversation you are in dramatically increases your ability to produce clarity and effectiveness in any meeting you attend and particularly those for the purpose of executing breakthrough projects.

Managing Conversational Direction

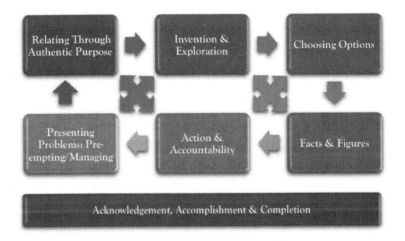

Each Intentional Authentic Dialogue has a specific purpose:

Relating through Authentic Purpose starts with each person authentically sharing the purpose they believe they are here to fulfill on in this life as a unique self; their background including any relevant information which would have the group relate to them in a common way; what their relationship to the project is; how they became a part of the project, etc. Essentially setting the foundation for all interactions.

Invention and Exploration encompasses sharing your commitment to what is possible in the project; inventing ideas for the project; allowing for the exploration of the most outrageous and inconceivable possibilities and considering alternatives and more alternatives.

Choosing Options requires selecting ideas from the invention and exploration dialogue to potentially move forward on; ranking the ideas in order of aligned on attractiveness to the group; choosing, shaping and tailoring these ideas for implementation.

Facts and Figures are related to verifiable experiences. For example, "X result will be hit by Y timeframe". And when asked, "Did you achieve your quarterly commitment of $250,000 in cost reductions?" The answer is yes or no, not "Well, this is why the targets weren't hit..." and a 20 minute explanation.

Action and Accountability refers to commitments in time as to who is going to do what by when.

Presenting Problems: Pre-empting/Managing and Resolving points out potential difficulties and presenting problems and engages in resolving these presenting problems as opportunities once they arise.

Acknowledgment, Accomplishment, and Completion includes acknowledging the accomplishment of the team; distinguishing what worked and didn't work; determining what can be learned from such knowledge and formally declaring the project complete.

In addition to managing these Intentional Authentic Dialogues, there also seem to be useful "Intentional Word Actions" that when used help create clarity and purpose inside of the Intentional Authentic Dialogues. Intentional Word Actions are most effectively designed in the form of a fundamental "word or words" that signifies clear committed action. Word actions could be articulated as claims, proclamations, affirmations of commitment, requests, inventing possibilities, considering options, inviting,

⌒ Intentional Word Actions
  ⌒ Claim
  ⌒ Proclamation
  ⌒ Commitment
  ⌒ Stand Accountable
  ⌒ Request
  ⌒ Invent
  ⌒ Assess
  ⌒ Consider
  ⌒ Invite
  ⌒ Acknowledge

directing, or promising. You and your team can create whatever "word actions" provide clarity and responsiveness. The key is to align on them and to honor the use of them with rigorous integrity.

For example, let's look at a category of Intentional Word Actions that has worked for groups I have coached in the past called a "claim." A claim as it is defined here is a type of commitment in which known evidence exists to support the claim. That is, the commitment inferred in the claim is to provide validating evidence for the claim. For example: "The project is on schedule." "I met my sales quota." "We will increase revenue by 10% this year which is a 2% increase from last year." If you stop and take the time to notice the dialogues around you in your office, claims tend to be a basic way people communicate. They are based on inferred evidence from the past. While these sorts of commitments are necessary and useful, claims are distinct from the type of commitments necessary for breakthrough. Since one cannot produce evidence from the future (unless you are Michael J Fox, i.e., "Back to the Future"), breakthroughs cannot be claimed.

A different way to clearly articulate a commitment to a breakthrough is required, something not based on the past - like perhaps a "proclamation". A proclamation is more of an announcement of one's intention to fulfill on a commitment promised for an entirely unpredictable outcome from the future. While a proclamation does consider the past it is not held hostage to "predetermined" notions of the past regarding what may or may not be possible. Committing to an unprecedented result could be said to be making a proclamation that something "shall be", with consideration of the past however also regardless of the past. Becoming an authentic leader demands that one learn how to manage this paradoxical thinking. The authentic leader has to learn how to manage the gap between "knowing" how something will be fulfilled on tactically, i.e., through a created plan, and "knowing" committedly through a deep conviction that something will be fulfilled on via the integrity of the person's word related to a passionate, responsibly "owned" commitment.

A great example of an authentic leader managing this paradox is the breakthrough space mission of Apollo 13. Eugene Kranz as the mission control commander made the proclamation that "failure was not an option" when faced with the dire presenting problem of bringing the space shuttle 13 and it's crew safely back to earth after a catastrophic explosion on board the aircraft. Initially there was no workable plan to accomplish this nor was there any evidence that it was remotely possible. Yet Kranz's proclamation was the source of an unprecedented national "breakthrough project", and Apollo 13 against all odds was brought safely home. This real life scenario truly captures the essence of an authentic leader standing for a breakthrough in the face of "no agreement". Another well known example which could be categorized in this vein of thinking was in the 1960's when President John F. Kennedy committed the United States to a 10-year time frame for successfully putting astronauts on the moon and bringing them home safely when there was absolutely no "known" evidence that this could conceivably be accomplished.

These examples highlight that while on your authentic leadership development journey, it is important not fall prey to another's misinterpretation of a proclamation for a claim. When an organization unfamiliar with the concept of breakthrough is introduced to the distinction, my experience has been that less than open-minded individuals will misinterpret a proclamation for a claim and proceed to engage in a campaign to kill the possibility of the proclamation based on the fact that no evidence exists to validate that the breakthrough is possible looking from the past. This has happened over and over again in my client engagements (and in the history of any commitment to innovation in general for that matter). Therefore, do not be alarmed; this is a normal, "business as usual" reaction from people unfamiliar with operating at the level of authentic leadership and breakthrough thinking.

To address this to some degree, after a proclamation is made, a structure needs to be created that provides a notion of how you and your team conceive of fulfilling on the proclamation. This initial implementation plan won't ever fully "play out" exactly as designed but it does at least allow for an initial line of sight, created from the future breakthrough accomplishment fulfilled, which you and your team can follow and adjust to during the implementation process. This initial plan won't fully satisfy the zealously committed cynic uninterested in transforming anything but it will give you and your team the initial clarity needed to move forward on the breakthrough commitment.

While this new framework for communication in the form of "Intentional Authentic Dialogues" and "Intentional Word Actions" may initially seem like simply semantics or occur "odd", cumbersome to create, remember and use, one must keep in mind that all specializations have their <u>own language</u> in order for the professionals in those specializations to communicate and perform at optimal levels, e.g., engineers, architects, surgeons, financial planners, police officers, academic researchers, chefs, etc. Authentic leaders are no exception. Words are necessary for the formation of thought. The vocabulary of Intentional Word Actions and the categories of Intentional Authentic Dialogues are necessary for the effective execution of clearly articulated thinking as it relates to authentic leadership for the purpose of causing breakthrough performance. Your current conversational design is giving you the results you presently have. If you want different results, you must alter the framework and execution of the design.

Thinking and speaking is a reflection of your priorities and attitude toward life. Because of the uncomfortable nature of being clear, responsible and accountable for one's speaking, many will tend to diminish the rigor that it takes to develop and implement this framework for conversation as action, often simplistically asserting that to be authentic and lead, one "Just needs to do the right thing!" My response to that is "The right thing for whom?" This line of overly simplified thinking seems to be used as a defense mechanism by an undisciplined and uncommitted "self" living in a fantasy world of irresponsibility, false hope and self-righteousness (i.e., <u>*you*</u> know what the "right thing" is and <u>*"they" don't*</u>). Reveling in the fog of "business as usual" ways of communicating and allowing people to hide in the shadows is not a demonstration of authentic leadership. Creating, aligning on and consistently using a clearly defined framework for effective communication designed for action shows an authentic leader's commitment to strategic thinking, transparency and integrity.

The Paradoxes of Intentional Authentic Dialogue: Overcoming "Cordial Duplicity"

One meaning of "to communicate" is "to make something common," i.e., to convey information or knowledge from one person to another in as accurate a way as possible. This meaning is certainly appropriate in a myriad of contexts. Many Intentional Word Actions could fall into this category, for example articulating a commitment, a promise, or a request. Nevertheless, this meaning does not cover all that encompasses communication. For example, when you are in a dialogue you typically do not respond to another person with exactly the same meaning in which that person intends to relay in his or her speaking. When a person replies to something you have said, you tend to notice the difference between what you meant to say and what the person understood.

If you are willing to consider what this difference brings to the conversation then you may be able to see something new, which is relevant both to your own views and the views of the other person. There literally can be a continual emergence of a new content that becomes common to both of you. Therefore, in contrast to some Intentional Word Actions (IWA) used to *make common* certain ideas or items of information that are already known to the two parties, often in Intentional Authentic Dialogues (IAD), two people are making something *in common*, i.e., creating something new together. This type of communication, leading to the creation of something new, can only be had if people are able to openly listen to each other without trying to influence each other. In this way IAD proposes several paradoxes.

Each person involved has to be primarily interested in truth and coherence, so that he is ready to drop old ideas and let go of dug in positions, and be equally ready to go on to something different, when this is called for. The antithesis of this type of interaction tends to promote and perpetuate "cordial duplicity". That is to say, it's better to be "nice" or "professional" and **pretend to agree** or **be fully engaged** in the dialogue to a person's face, while reserving the right to internally assess them as wrong and in worse case scenarios, an idiot! If the mind treats a paradox (a difference of opinion) as a "real problem" to be solved, then since the paradox by definition has "no solution" the mind is virtually caught in a terminal loop. *Someone has to be right* and *someone has to be wrong* so people often default to "cordial duplicity", simply smiling and not saying anything authentic to forward the conversation or inauthentically pretending to agree with the person.

If two people merely want to convey certain ideas or points of view to each other, they must inevitably fail to engage in Intentional Authentic Dialogue for the purpose of creating something new *in common*. Each person will hear the other through the filter of his own positional thoughts, maintaining and defending them, regardless of whether or not they are coherent or help to resolve an issue at hand. The interaction will inevitably result in just the sort of confusion that leads to the conundrum of never ending "problems in communication" so prevalent in our organizations today.

A Possibility

All knowledge is limited, because it is an abstraction (only a part) of the whole. It consists only of what we have learned up to that point. Therefore, knowledge always has the possibility of being incomplete. If one's attitude is flexible, committed to coherence and workability, one might say, "Okay, I acknowledge the incoherence. I will let go of my inflexible position regarding past knowledge. Let's see what new things I can discover." This way, the person has an opportunity to find out what is missing in their current knowledge base and to build on that. Fundamentally there is no reason to defend knowledge. It either is workable or it's not. But people are caught up defending it all the time.

If people are to cooperate and work together they have to be able to create something **in common**, something that takes shape in their mutual discussions and actions. Recent developments in both quantum theory and cognitive science make strong cases to support the proposition that perceiving the world in terms of separate fragments is an inaccurate way of thinking. We have divided our world into numerous isolated bits that seem to have no connection to one another. This is no more evident than when one observes the inability of specialists in different fields to talk across specialties. Rather than reason together, people tend to defend their "territory".

Engaging in Intentional Authentic Dialogues is one potentially powerful process of inquiry to forward collective learning and thought. It provides an alternative to "business as usual" ways of being in communication by focusing our attention, not on problems as they are initially interpreted but on our fundamental habits of thought, assumptions and unintentional ways of speaking behind our traditional problem solving, and thinking. By exploring these concepts, one may also find ways of transforming the self-and-world view from which all of our thinking and behavior emerges and more effectively identify the kinds of habitual errors in thinking we may be perpetuating. These errors ultimately stop authentic inquiry and our possibility as human beings of engaging in extraordinary breakthrough behavior as individuals and in groups.

Components of a Breakthrough Project

- Objective
- Results to be Accomplished
- Description & Scope
- Key Processes Impacted
- Assumptions, Constraints, Risks
- Team Members & Stakeholders
- Milestones & Timeline

Objective

○ An inspiring well crafted vision statement articulating the purpose of the project.

○ Why are we doing this?
○ How will this significantly impact our business?
○ What difference does it make for me?
○ Why operate differently than we already are?

Results to be Accomplished

○ What are the outcomes committed to and by when will they be achieved? ...X by Y.

○ How will we measure accomplishment of the results?

○ What are the specific metrics to be achieved in each area impacted?

○ What is the impact on the operation, i.e., reduction on losses, time or money saved, minimization of errors, increase in production?

Description & Scope

o What work must be performed to deliver the result?

o What are the boundaries of the work?

o What areas of the organization will be impacted?

o What resources are needed: time, money, approvals, new technology?

Key Processes Impacted/
Assumptions, Constraints and Risks

○ What operating processes will be impacted?

○ Whose work processes will need to be altered?

○ What are the assumed conditions?

○ Are there extreme constraints?

○ What are the risks?

Team Members and Stakeholders

○ Who will be the sponsor for the project?

○ Who will lead the project?

○ Who are the key people who will also need to be involved?

○ Does the project require input from other areas of the organization?

○ Does the team have diversity including hourly workers, salary, supervisory, administrative, etc.?

○ Is technical expertise required?

○ Are the people on the team effected by the implementation and outcome of the project?

Milestones and Timelines

○ What milestones need to be accomplished and by when?

○ What are the conversations which need to be managed and the steps which need to be taken by what dates for this to happen?

○ When and how will progress in the project be reviewed?

Putting it All Together

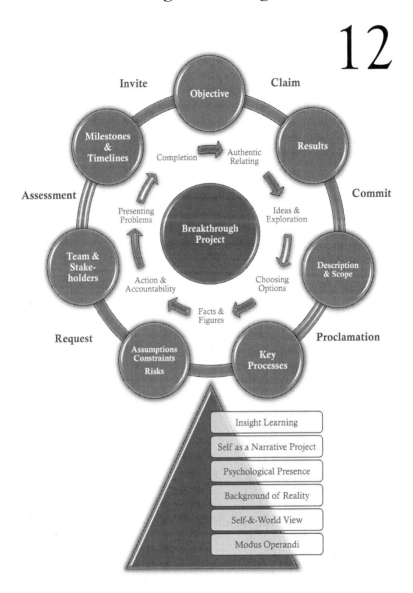

Authentic Leadership Development Model

If You Choose Authentic Leadership...
Congratulations!

In our society today, we have the most over-informed, under-reflective people in the history of civilization. Perhaps, if you choose to develop yourself in becoming an authentic leader you can join me in disrupting and transforming the existing processes in our organizations that perpetuate a lack of psychological presence, ethical deterioration and prevent authenticity, self-reflection, and learning. If you choose Authentic Leadership Development for yourself and/or your organization...Congratulations! It is an amazingly rewarding journey!

"Therefore you must always keep in mind that a path is only a path; if you feel you should not follow it, you must not stay with it under any conditions.... Does this path have a heart? If it does, the path is good; if it doesn't, it is of no use. Both paths lead nowhere; but one has a heart, the other doesn't. One makes for a joyful journey; as long as you follow it, you are one with it. The other will make you curse your life. One makes you strong; the other weakens you."
Don Juan [1]

[1] Casteneda, C. (1968). The teachings of Don Juan: A Yaqui Way of Knowledge. University of California Press.

About the Author

Pauline Serice is president and CEO of Pauline Serice & Associates, Inc. located in Houston, Texas. She is responsible for the creation and execution of this successfully unique authentic leadership development and change management consulting company. Her specialization is authentic leadership development coaching and change management consulting where breakthroughs in being in authentic communication and collaboration are essential to success. Ms. Serice's experience includes producing breakthrough results with an international transformational development company as their Communication Program Manager and as a Sr. Manager of Change Management for a major international food distribution company. In addition, she has extensive experience in the behavioral health field working as a Sr. Behaviorist with the Houston Medical Association implementing a successful change-intervention program for the morbidly obese.

Over the past 16 years, Ms. Serice has worked with a diverse clientele both nationally and internationally which encompasses such industries as healthcare, manufacturing, oil and gas, shipping, financial services, food distribution, hospitality, retail, pharmaceutical and horticultural landscaping. She received her undergraduate BFA degree and graduate Industrial and Organizational Psychology MS degree, from Louisiana Tech University and Capella University, respectively and is currently a PhD candidate completing research with Capella University specializing in Authentic Leadership Psychology.

For more information contact:
E-mail: Pauline@paulineserice.com
Website: www.paulineserice.com

INSIGHTS

NOTES

INSIGHTS

NOTES

INSIGHTS

NOTES